THE INDUSTRIAL REVOLUTION

Volume 8

America's Second Industrial Revolution

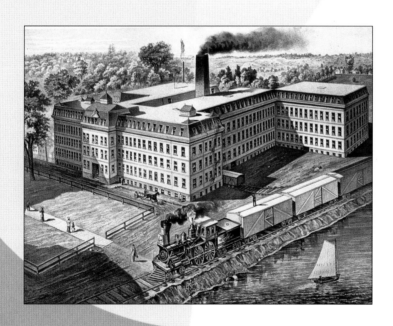

James R. Arnold & Roberta Wiener

Grolier

An imprint of Scholastic Library Publishing
Danbury, Connecticut

First published in 2005 by Grolier
An imprint of Scholastic Library Publishing
Old Sherman Turnpike
Danbury, Connecticut 06816

For information address the publisher:
Scholastic Library Publishing, Old Sherman Turnpike,
Danbury, Connecticut 06816

Library of Congress Cataloging-in-Publication Data

Arnold, James R.
   The industrial revolution / James R. Arnold and Roberta Wiener.
      p. cm
   Includes bibliographical references and index.
   Contents: v. 1. A turning point in history – v. 2. The industrial
revolution begins – v. 3. The industrial revolution spreads – v. 4. The
industrial revolution comes to America – v. 5. The growth of the
industrial revolution in America – v. 6. The industrial revolution
spreads through Europe – v. 7. The worldwide industrial revolution –
v. 8. America's second industrial revolution – v. 9. The industrial
revolution and the working class v. 10. The industrial revolution and
American society.
      ISBN 0-7172-6031-3 (set)—ISBN 0-7172-6032-1 (v. 1)—
   ISBN 0-7172-6033-X (v. 2)—ISBN 0-7172-6034-8 (v. 3)—
   ISBN 0-7172-6035-6 (v. 4)—ISBN 0-7172-6036-4 (v. 5)—
   ISBN 0-7172-6037-2 (v. 6)—ISBN 0-7172-6038-0 (v. 7)—
   ISBN 0-7172-6039-9 (v. 8)—ISBN 0-7172-6040-2 (v. 9)—
   ISBN 0-7172-6041-0 (v. 10)
      1. Industrial revolution. 2. Economic history. I. Wiener, Roberta.
   II. Title.

   HD2321.A73 2005
   330.9'034–dc22   2004054243

Printed and bound in China

CONTENTS

INTRODUCTION

The discovery of oil deposits in Pennsylvania and immense soft coal reserves in Pennsylvania and nearby states began a second Industrial Revolution in the United States during the 1850s. The expansion of the nation's railroad system also stimulated industrial development.

Railroad construction directly spurred economic growth by creating tremendous demand for iron and steel, locomotives, and railroad cars. Railroad construction also had great secondary effects by boosting demand for coal and for machine tools. As a result, large-scale coke smelting, steel-making, and heavy-machinery construction grew in the area spanning from Pittsburgh to Cleveland between 1850 and

Soon after the 1859 discovery of oil in Titusville, the search for oil accelerated elsewhere in northwestern Pennsylvania. Oil wells at Oil Creek, Pennsylvania, in 1864.

1880, and then south of Lake Michigan around 1900. Furthermore, as the railroads began linking more and more places, producers found that they could sell to distant markets, fueling more growth.

Left: In an earlier era colonial ironworks depended on huge draft horses to haul iron ore and pig iron in freight wagons.

Below: Railroad construction created enormous demand for iron, and later, steel. An iron railroad bridge spanning an American river.

Chicago greatly benefitted from the nation's expanding rail net. In 1853 rail lines connected Chicago with the East. One year later railways linked Chicago with St. Louis. Three years later the first railroad bridge spanned the Mississippi River at Davenport, Iowa. Between 1860 and 1875 four large railroads completed projects to connect Chicago with the Atlantic coast. Because of the railroads Chicago grew rapidly from a modest prairie town to a booming commercial city.

The Civil War interrupted America's rail expansion, but after the war it continued at a tremendous pace. After the war two companies immediately began building lines to create a transcontinental railroad. The Union Pacific Railroad extended its line westward, while the Central Pacific Railroad began setting track from San Francisco eastward. The great moment arrived in 1869 at Promontory Point, Utah, when the two lines met. The ceremonial driving of a golden spike to complete the first transcontinental railroad was more than a symbolic act. After that three additional lines were built to span the continent, and new north-south lines branched off them to connect urban centers from Minneapolis to Kansas City to Houston. In 1872 alone, workers built over 7,400 miles of track, a record total never surpassed.

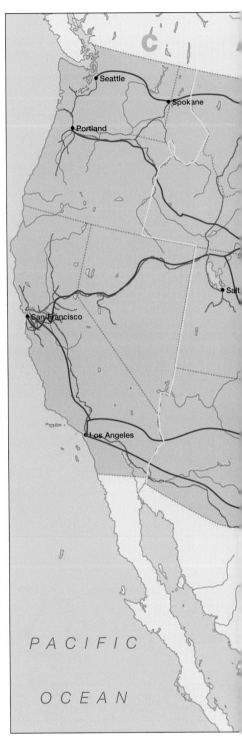

Above: The completion of the transcontinental railroad (left) in 1869 was only the beginning. Among the new transcontinental lines was the Great Northern Railway connecting Minneapolis with the Pacific Northwest. It allowed the delivery of wheat from the Pacific Northwest to urban consumers along both the West and East coasts, and opened the region's vast timber resources to the national market.

Early railroads:
See also
Volume 5 pages 28–41

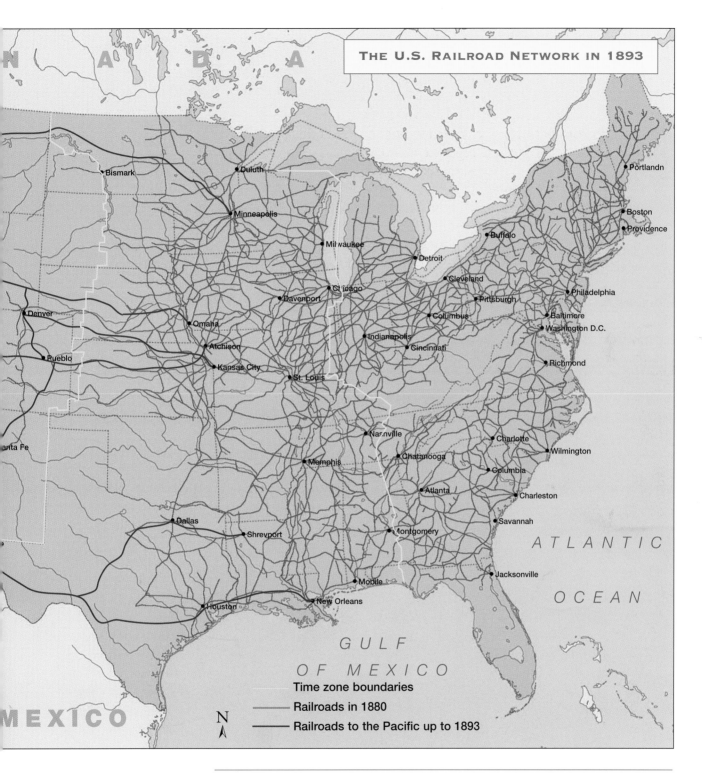

THE U.S. RAILROAD NETWORK IN 1893

Time zone boundaries
Railroads in 1880
Railroads to the Pacific up to 1893

N

In 1870 the United States had nearly 53,000 miles of railroad track. Ten years later that number had risen to more than 93,000. By 1890 more than 167,000 miles of track covered the United States. The tremendous expansion of railroads created complex scheduling challenges. To help solve them, the nation adopted standard times zones in 1883. They typified the drive toward standardization and uniformity in many aspects of life.

MECHANIZATION CHANGES THE LAND

Early loggers in action. An axeman fells a tree while the whipsaw team saws a felled tree into logs.

The completion of the first transcontinental railroad marked the beginning of a truly national market in the United States. Western raw materials sped eastward along iron rails, and manufactured products from the east traveled westward to meet the needs of the West's growing population.

THE WEST COAST LUMBER INDUSTRY

During the first years of European settlement along the West Coast individuals felled trees with axes and used the handheld whipsaw to make boards and planks. Lumber production was labor-intensive, hard work. The first steam-powered sawmill was built north of San Francisco in 1844; but most mills relied on water power, and all used old-fashioned saw designs. Efficient exploitation of the Pacific Northwest's abundant timber stands required new tools.

One such tool was the circular saw, which was introduced to the West around 1857. In that year one mill on Puget Sound, in Washington State, had a giant circular saw with a blade 6.5 feet in diameter. However, circular saws could only cut through a log with a diameter of not more than half that of the saw itself. Furthermore, the giant saws could not operate at high speeds.

Given the size of the region's giant redwoods and Douglas firs, this was a serious constraint.

Technical solutions—such as the double circular saw with one blade set above the other—began appearing in the 1870s. Nathan Spaulding began manufacturing circular saws in Sacramento, California, and patented a saw design with replaceable teeth that soon became the standard. The next improvement in saws appeared in 1885—giant band saws, each equipped with a thin loop of toothed steel that could cut planks up to 80 inches wide.

Also in the 1880s lumberjacks began using long crosscut saws instead of axes to fell standing timber, thereby reducing felling time by 80 percent. Between 1870 and 1900 the mechanization of the timber industry caused West Coast lumber production to increase almost sixfold.

This had some important environmental consequences. Mills routinely dumped waste sawdust in the ocean. The waste accumulated and blocked shipping channels. The Army Corps of Engineers had to dredge the channels, and that chore led to legislation banning the dumping of such waste. Almost a century later the corps cited that precedent for justification to assume its modern regulatory role in water pollution. Also, the

A fallen giant in the Cascade Mountains of Washington State, 1899.

rapid depletion of the forest led to one of the first federal conservation measures, the Forest Reserve Act of 1891.

MINING IN THE WEST

The famous Gold Rush of 1849 brought thousands of miners to California. To extract the gold, miners developed new approaches, including hydraulic mining. Hydraulic mining, begun in 1852, was essentially a form of mass production. Workers built dams in the high Sierra Mountains and brought the water to the work site at the mountain's base through a network of ditches, **flumes**, and pipes. The descending water flow created high pressure that workers directed through nozzles against the mountainside. The high pressure collapsed the mountain's face into a **slurry** that went through **sluice**s to collect the gold.

Hydraulic mining required vast amounts of water—some 200 million parts of water to obtain one part of gold. By 1867 capitalists had financed over 300 separate hydraulic systems with more than 6,000 miles of ditches through the mountains. Hydraulic mining was so capital intensive that by the 1880s some $100 million had been invested.

Although the technology and infrastructure of hydraulic mining were eventually applied to irrigation districts, municipal waterworks, and hydroelectric systems, at the time

FLUME: a ditch or trough that carries water down a mountainside; similar to a sluice

SLUICE: a ditch or trough that carries slurry from a mine site to the point where miners extract the ore

SLURRY: mixture of water and soil

A Washington State forest after the lumberjacks had done their work. The loss of trees left the land ready to erode with the next heavy rainfall.

Right: Hydraulic mining: water cannons blasting away at the soil in 1866.

Below: Between the end of the Revolutionary War and the beginning of the Civil War the population of the United States grew from 3.9 million to 31.4 million. By 1860 some 4.5 million Americans, or 14% of the national population, lived west of the Mississippi River. Ten years later that number had grown to 6.9 million and 18% of the total. By 1870, according to the official census, more than 37,000 "manufacturing establishments" were located west of the Mississippi.

THE U.S. IN 1861

CANADA

WASHINGTON TERRITORY

DAKOTA TERRITORY

MINNESOTA

MAINE

VERMONT

NEW HAMPSHIRE

MASSACHUSETTS

OREGON

WISCONSIN

NEW YORK

RHODE ISLAND

CONNECTICUT

MICHIGAN

NEBRASKA TERRITORY

PENNSYLVANIA

NEW JERSEY

NEVADA TERRITORY

IOWA

OHIO

INDIANA

WASHINGTON D.C.

DELAWARE

ILLINOIS

WEST VIRGINIA

MARYLAND

UTAH TERRITORY

COLORADO TERRITORY

VIRGINIA

CALIFORNIA

KANSAS

MISSOURI

KENTUCKY

NORTH CAROLINA

TENNESSEE

SOUTH CAROLINA

NEW MEXICO TERRITORY

Indian Territory (unorganized

ARKANSAS

ALABAMA

GEORGIA

ATLANTIC

PACIFIC OCEAN

OCEAN

MISSISSIPPI

MISSISSIPPI

TEXAS

LOUISIANA

FLORIDA

N

GULF OF MEXICO

MEXICO

● Territories
● Free States
● Slave States

11

An 1878 view showing how hydraulic mining changed the landscape.

hydraulic mining was enormously destructive of the environment. The removal of entire mountain faces caused massive erosion. Eroded material and mining debris silted and clogged downstream rivers, which in turn caused flooding.

The California legislature established the office of state engineer in 1878. One of his major concerns was dealing with the problems caused by hydraulic mining. However, the courts acted first by effectively banning the industry because it was too destructive. The action by the U.S. Circuit Court in 1884 marked an important, early intervention by the courts into environmental law.

Opposite: An 1876 cutaway view of the Comstock mine showing how timber "square sets" supported the underground chambers.

THE COMSTOCK SILVER MINES

After the California Gold Rush miners fanned out all over the West to search for gold and silver. Western silver mining required new techniques that originated with the international industrial community. A German engineer introduced a system of timber wall and ceiling supports, called "square sets," to prevent cave-ins in the underground chambers of mines. After that square sets spread worldwide for use wherever mining took place in soft, crumbling earth. Working deep underground, miners encountered temperatures as high as 170

degrees Fahrenheit. American technicians installed large pumps to deliver ice water to the miners and blowers to provide ventilation. The miners used French-designed compressed-air drills and diamond-studded rotary drills. They opened new

Right: Electric power transformed the underground mining industry. A description of electricity use at a Colorado mine in 1900 related that a miner "may go up to his work from town on an electric car, go down in the mine by an electric hoist, operated by electric signals, the shaft being kept dry by an electric pump, do his work by an electric light, talk to the town and thence to the world by an electric telephone, run a drill electrically operated, and fire shots [of explosives] by an electric blast." The pumping engine at the Comstock mine.

shafts with the Swedish inventor Alfred Nobel's dynamite and nitroglycerine. To extract the silver, technicians took advantage of Mexico's long history of silver mining to mechanize a Mexican process.

By the 1870s about 3,000 miners worked some 190 miles of shafts in the Comstock Mines of Nevada. Comstock was the training ground for technicians and miners who later spread throughout the West to exploit everything from quartz in California to silver in Colorado.

The use of electricity in mines—for light, ventilation, and transport—and the introduction of mechanical drilling revolutionized underground mining in the West. Between 1880 and 1902 worker productivity nearly doubled. What did not change was the danger. Statistics showed that 1.7 English miners were killed per 1,000 employed, while in Colorado the figure was 5.96 and in Montana a staggering 8.28.

Above: Alfred Nobel invented dynamite, which he patented in 1868. Dynamite was a great improvement over the extremely dangerous nitroglycerine. After an explosion at his nitroglycerine plant in Sweden killed his brother, Nobel combined liquid nitroglycerine with a stable dry material so that it would not explode until the fuse was lit. Nobel's will directed that his fortune be used to establish the Nobel Prize, which began in 1901.

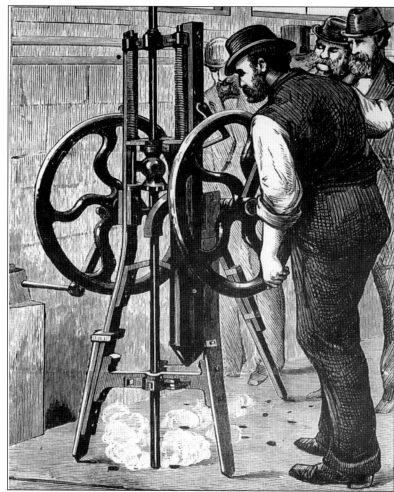

Right: Exhibitions such as the Centennial Exposition in Philadelphia showcased the latest technology. A newer version of a rock drill on display in 1876.

Left: In 1870 the inventor, Charles Burleigh, demonstrated an electric-powered drill in Colorado. The ability to drill through hard rock revolutionized mining in the West. Burleigh drills at work in the Comstock mine.

Below: In the 1840s coal started its climb to become the fuel of choice for industrial America. But it came at a price. The dangers of underground mining in the West were so great that organizations like the Miners' Union at the Comstock Mine in 1867 and the Western Federation of Miners, formed in Colorado in 1893, militantly worked for better conditions and higher wages. An American newspaper portrays the aftermath of an 1878 coal mine explosion.

THE MECHANIZATION OF FARMING

The first European colonists of the 1600s and the American farmer of the 1840s shared many of the same tasks. They used hand tools to chop down trees, cleared troublesome stumps with teams of oxen, broke the soil with simple iron-reinforced wood plows, and planted and harvested by hand. The work was hard and slow. As late as 1841 a typical Massachusetts farmer

An American farmer in the 1880s faces the daunting task of plowing a weed-choked field to prepare it for the new growing season.

had to spend 13 days to clear the stumps from one acre of land. Plowing alone accounted for 60 percent of the labor involved in raising grain.

When settlers moved west, they encountered vast prairies that presented new challenges. Farmers had to break the dense mass of roots that characterized lush prairie grass and confront the tendency of moist prairie soils to stick to the plow's moldboard. The solution was the so-called "steel" plow, which

Above and bottom: In 1837 John Deere manufactured his first "steel" plow. An early plow clad in metal strips and an iron plow with a steel edge.

Right: More than four in five American workers labored in agriculture in 1800, but by the year 2000 the number had fallen to fewer than one in twenty. Reaping hay by hand.

used strips of steel attached to the moldboard's face to prevent soil from sticking and had the strength to break up thick prairie sod.

Haymaking was also laborious and time consuming. A farmer spent a day cutting by hand an acre of hay and another half day to arrange the cut grass into windrows so it could dry. As early as the late eighteenth century tinkerers made horse-drawn drag rakes out of wood to gather hay into windrows. By the 1850s these devices had evolved into lightweight, spring-toothed, self-dumping hay rakes (a spring allowed the metal teeth to give way when they encountered too much resistance and so avoided the teeth breaking or the rake getting stuck). These rakes were tremendous labor savers. Depending on the weight of the grass, a single driver and a single horse could gather between 20 and 30 acres of hay a day.

Inventors and tinkerers had long tried to meet the challenge of harvesting grains. Cyrus McCormick learned from the efforts of tinkerers including his father and used his knowledge to develop a horse-drawn reaper that he patented in 1854. The McCormick reaper was the century's most important agricultural machine. It revolutionized farming and allowed farming operations to expand over a vast region extending from western Minnesota south through Iowa, Kansas, and into Texas. Because of mechanization the amount of farm land

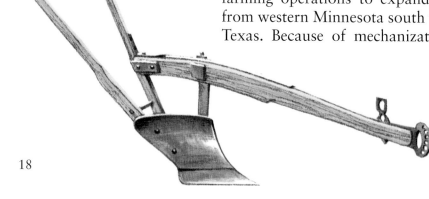

Cyrus McCormick's horse-drawn reaper changed agriculture. Demonstrations of his invention keenly interested members of the public.

more than doubled between 1850 and 1890, and continued to increase dramatically until 1910.

Wheat was the great crop grown by most farmers in the Midwest, across the prairies, and in the far west. By 1880 each of the steps necessary to bring a wheat crop to market had been improved with the development of new tools and machines. Farmers used iron plows (often made by the John Deere Company) or gang plows, which could work more than one row at a time. They used automatic planters and cultivated the soil with spring-toothed harrows that tripped instead of sticking when they encountered roots or rocks. Large combines, some pulled by up to 21 mules, cut, threshed, and bound the wheat in one pass.

All of that equipment was costly, but rural banks proved more than willing to lend large sums to farmers who wanted to modernize. In turn, the farmers' motivation was the enormous labor savings that mechanization offered. Before mechanization each bushel of harvested wheat required 61 hours of labor; after, only three. Mechanization also allowed farmers to work much more acreage.

Before mechanization farmers grew a variety of crops to feed their own families. However, the new equipment tended to be

19

Above: A 30-horse combine quickly performed work once done by hand, but maintaining and hitching up all the horses also required time and effort.

single-purpose machines suitable for one crop but not another. Furthermore, because mechanization was far more capital intensive, farmers, and the banks that loaned them money sought higher returns on their investment. The new emphasis was not to provide for one's own family's needs but rather to

Children planting beans on their family's Midwestern farm in the early twentieth century.

Opposite: During the nineteenth century animals provided the power for most farm machines. Steam, internal combustion engines, and electricity became more widely used as the century drew to a close, but horse power still dominated. A horse-drawn cultivator in the early twentieth century.

grow what the market wanted. Accordingly, after identifying market demand, farmers switched to monoculture (the growing of one crop) to increase profit. Monoculture later proved to have adverse environmental effects, but at the time it was a logical economic choice.

A much more immediate result caused by the mechanization of farming was a tremendous increase in the number of acres put to agriculture. Simultaneously, the percentage of the population working in agriculture declined. Laborsaving machines meant that fewer workers could raise and harvest more crops. In 1820 each farm worker produced enough food to feed 4.1 people. By 1900 one worker could feed seven people. After the Civil War increasing numbers of rural people left their farms to seek work in urban areas. This usually meant taking a factory job.

In addition, the mechanization of agriculture led to declining prices for farm products. For example, the price of wheat fell from $2.06 per bushel in 1866 to 95 cents in 1874 and to 45 cents after the depression of 1893. Falling prices led to human misery, particularly among the less well-off, who often had to sell their family farms. It also caused political unrest among rural people and the birth of new social and political organizations such as the Grange (a farmer's organization established in 1867), the Farmers Alliance movement, which had over one million members in 1890, and eventually new political parties such as the Populist Party.

For rural people the mechanization of farming provided both advantages and unforeseen disadvantages. For urban dwellers it was pure advantage since food prices fell dramatically. Ahead lay an even more mechanized future as, inevitably, inventors sought to replace horsepower with mechanical power.

The first self-steering, self-propelled traction steam engine appeared in 1882. The use of steam expanded until 1913, at which time some 10,000 steam engines were in use on American farms. But the more convenient internal combustion engines were clearly the machines of choice and came to dominate the mechanized future. The early twentieth century brought electricity and tractors to most American farms. One consequence was the end of a 300-year-old tradition of small,

A steam-powered plow in 1908.

A 1914 tractor powered by a gasoline-fueled internal combustion engine.

family-owned farms and their replacement by large-scale, capital-intensive agricultural practices.

The mechanization of farming also had another important social consequence. When farming had been more labor intensive, most farm workers were like apprentice farmers. Farmers generally treated them as part of the family. A machine like the self-binding harvester (introduced in 1878) slashed labor needs for grain harvesting by three-quarters. Farmers no longer needed so many full-time workers. Furthermore, before mechanization farmers usually shared the heavy labor with their hired help. After, farmers typically did the lighter physical work while the part-time workers did the harder labor. The widening gulf between farmers and their hired helpers led to a permanent class of part-time and migrant workers. Society began to look down at part-time farm laborers, calling them "tramps" and, worse, treating them poorly and offering them low wages.

In the 1870s a Midwestern farm worker asked, "while the improved machinery is gathering our large crops, making our boots and shoes, doing the work of our carpenters, stone sawyers, and builders, thousands of able, willing men are going from place to place seeking employment and finding none. The question naturally arises, is improved machinery a blessing or a curse?"

A NEW TOOL FOR WORKING AT HOME

The mechanization of the textile industry brought consumers cheap cotton and woolen cloth. However, retail clothing remained expensive because it required workers to sew patterned cloth together by hand. That dramatically changed in 1856 when Isaac Singer designed a sewing machine that combined ideas taken from prior inventions with his own inventions. He then steadily improved his invention until the name Singer became synonymous with the sewing machine itself.

Furthermore, Singer was much more than an inventor. He had the vision to see how his machine could be used both in the factory and at home. In a very modern manner he advertised heavily, provided instructional courses on how to use his machine, offered financing for its purchase on an installment plan, and was the first to promote a sales and service contract.

Individual seamstresses and tailors could hardly compete with machine-made clothes. Instead, they had to operate sewing machines in a sweatshop environment. At the same time, the machine brought back the putting out system. A home worker using a sewing machine could enter the trade without having any special skills or without having to make a large initial investment. Moreover, in the United States the flood of immigrants from central and eastern Europe provided an abundant source of low-cost labor willing to toil for long hours at the sewing machine.

The sewing machine also changed the traditional patterns of dress. In the past the wealthy purchased hand-tailored clothes, while the less well-off made their own clothes. By 1900 most consumers purchased machine-made clothes. Even members of the working class could often afford a Sunday suit for special occasions.

Left: In the days before the sewing machine shoes had been made by hand. A New England shoemaker proudly reported in 1760 that his two young sons had made 14 pair of women's shoes in a single week.

Opposite: A sewing machine in use at a book bindery. Singer also sold some of his machines from storefront locations he called "Singer emporiums." They were clean, attractive stores with a cheery atmosphere that helped persuade millions of American women that they needed Singer sewing machines in their own homes. In 1875 the Singer Sewing Machine Manufacturing Company sold nearly 200,000 machines.

Below: Shoe factories came to rely on machines to stitch the leather uppers to the soles. In 1870 factories in Lynn, Massachusetts, alone produced more than 11 million pair. An American shoe factory.

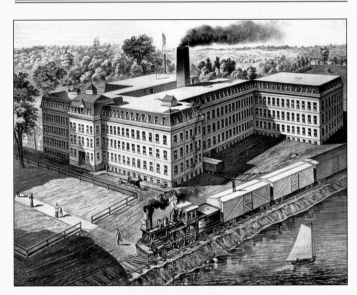

From an industrial viewpoint one of the beauties of an advance in mechanization was the potential to apply the invention or innovation to some other industry. For example, a machine designed to punch metal could easily be modified to punch leather. Likewise a coin-stamping machine could be converted to stamp metal panels for vehicles. So it was with Singer's invention. It gave birth to numerous related machines, including devices for button-holing, blind stitching, embroidery, and lace-making as well as applications in the glove-making, harness and saddle-making, book-binding, and boot and shoemaking industries.

THE RISE OF OIL

Since antiquity people had utilized petroleum when it appeared on the surface as an oil seep. Around the twelfth century the Arab invasion of Spain brought the secret of **distillation** to the western world. Thereafter petroleum, gathered from surface seeps, was used on a limited basis for lighting. Simultaneously, the Industrial Revolution brought increasing urbanization, which created demand for better illumination. In both Europe and North America kerosene, extracted from coal and also called coal oil, partially met this need.

> DISTILL: to purify a material by boiling and then cooling it, so that it condenses into a new container, leaving the impurities behind in the old container; to separate mixtures into their individual components

Whale oil provided the common fuel for lamps and lanterns until overhunting caused a steep decline in whale populations.

The machine tools on which the Industrial Revolution depended required lubricants to reduce friction and prevent overheating. This demand led to the search for convenient, cheap lubricants. Edwin Drake undertook the world's first successful drilling for the purpose of finding petroleum. In 1859 he struck oil in Titusville, in northwestern Pennsylvania. During 1859 the total U.S. production of oil was just 2,000 barrels, with each barrel holding 42 gallons. After Drake's success oil-drilling rigs spread like mushrooms to adjacent sites, and soon cheap oil, processed at existing coal oil refineries, became widely available. By the end of 1860 Pennsylvania production of oil rose to half a million barrels.

The American Civil War (1861-1865) created a booming

market for petroleum. Northern factories and machine shops expanded to meet government contracts, and these operations consumed lubricating and illuminating oil. Railroads likewise expanded operations in order to supply the army and move troops. Locomotives and freight and passenger cars needed constant lubrication. At the same time, the Confederate commerce-raiding ships interrupted whale oil supplies, the traditional source of lighting oil. By 1862 the North was producing about three million barrels of oil per year.

After the war industrial demand for oil continued to increase. A major bottleneck was in the transportation of oil. The oil wells in northwestern Pennsylvania were far from railroad lines and navigable waterways. Horse-drawn wagons loaded with wooden oil barrels moved the oil to railroads or to barge routes for transportation to refineries in distant cities such as Pittsburgh and Cleveland. Then the oil had to be moved to the consumer. The barrels were heavy, difficult to

The oil wells of Titusville, Pennsylvania, in 1860.

manipulate, and tended to leak, so the entire transportation process was inefficient.

The obvious solution was a pipeline. The first successful pipeline—made from welded, cast iron pipes two inches in diameter—opened in 1865. The line ran for six miles from an oil field to a railroad dock. Three pumping stations maintained pressure so that the line was able to move 80 barrels per hour. Within one year this short line had demonstrated its economic benefits and pointed the way to the future. During the next 25 years numerous new pipelines connected wells with nearby railroads (longer interstate and international pipelines were not built until the twentieth century).

Since railroads moved oil over long distances, the next breakthrough was the purpose-built tank car that could be loaded and unloaded from specially constructed railroad platforms. The telegraph complemented this

Above: The discovery of oil in America quickly captured the public imagination. As early as 1860, a picture of a Pennsylvania oil well adorned the cover of a songbook.

integrated system of pipelines and tanker cars. Managers could follow the progress of oil shipments from field to refinery and readily exploit market opportunities as supply and demand fluctuated. John D. Rockefeller saw more clearly than anyone else that the control of petroleum transportation would allow domination of the entire industry and yield fabulous profit.

By the turn of the century oil explorers had found "black gold" in 14 states as well as in Europe and the Far East. Production increased to 5.2 million barrels nationwide in 1870, 26.2 million in 1880, 45.8 million in 1890, and 63.6 million in 1900. The increase in supply led to new uses for oil and its derivatives. Various forms of petroleum served to lubricate specialized machines and tools. Kerosene heated indoor spaces, provided illumination in homes and factories, and was used as a fuel for cook stoves. And then, in the 1890s, the development of the internal combustion engine created a new demand for a special form of petroleum called gasoline.

Main picture and left: An oil pipeline and railroad tanker cars of the early twentieth century.

JOHN D. ROCKEFELLER

Born in Richford, New York, in 1839, Rockefeller grew up in Cleveland, Ohio. He had a strict Baptist upbringing that taught him exceptionally thrifty habits. After graduating from high school, he took a business course and began working as a clerk and bookkeeper. Rockefeller was just 20 years old when he learned about the world's first successful oil well in Titusville, Pennsylvania.

He immediately concluded that oil would play a major role in the economy and persuaded his boss to invest in oil refining. Within eight years he owned a controlling interest in the business, and by 1870 he incorporated his business as the Standard Oil Company. During the following two decades Rockefeller competed ruthlessly to build his company into the world's largest industrial firm. He built huge refineries that allowed him to take advantage of economies of scale. Independent producers could not compete and either went out of business or sold their assets to Rockefeller.

Rockefeller expanded the Standard Oil Company according to a vision he helped pioneer—the principle of vertical integration whereby a single business controls supply, production, shipping, and distribution. Vertical integration allowed deep cost cutting and boosted profit margins.

Standard Oil leased oil-rich properties, manufactured its own drilling equipment, and gained control of railroads and pipelines in order to keep transportation costs low. In addition, by 1882 Rockefeller had developed a new form of corporate organization using trusts and holding companies.

A trust was an arrangement in which stockholders exchanged with the board of trustees a controlling interest in their company and received trust certificates in return. After competing companies also performed this exchange, one board of trustees could make

decisions for all the companies. A holding company bought controlling interests in several companies that competed in a market (in Rockefeller's case, competing refineries). The holding company then set pricing rules and said who could sell what and where.

The goal of the trusts and holding companies was to squash competition and obtain monopoly control over the oil industry, and no one was more successful at this than Rockefeller. He gained control of hundreds of independent refineries. By 1890 the Standard Oil Company controlled over 70 percent of U.S. refining capacity, and John D. Rockefeller was one of the world's richest men.

People hated Rockefeller and other major industrialists for their extreme wealth and held them responsible for poverty among American workers. Journalists coined the phrase "robber barons" to describe them, saying the rich lived like royalty on the profits made by exploiting workers and hounding the competition out of business.

In 1890 the federal government passed the Sherman Antitrust Act, which outlawed industrial monopolies. A long legal wrangle ensued. Eventually the government prevailed, and Standard Oil broke into independent parts, including Exxon and Mobil.

Meanwhile, Rockefeller withdrew from company management and pursued his religious conviction that God expected the rich to spend their wealth to assist the needy. He donated hundreds of millions of dollars to charity, including millions to improve black education in the South, established the Rockefeller Foundation for educational, medical, and scientific research, and heavily funded the University of Chicago.

Because of these activities the public changed its view of Rockefeller from a ruthless robber baron to a respected philanthropist. In the decades to come, the view of all industrialists changed, and they were given credit for having modernized and enriched America.

A Standard Oil Refinery in Missouri. Crude petroleum is a mixture of oils of varying weights and characteristics. Refining involved heating crude petroleum in a large enclosed vat, producing volatile gases that condensed in a long outlet tube attached to the vat. The different portions (called fractions) of the condensed gases were then bottled and sent to market.

THE INTERNAL COMBUSTION ENGINE

Steam engines were external combustion engines in that they burned the fuel in a container (the boiler) that was separate from the engine, and a gas (the steam) communicated the energy from the boiler to the engine. By around the middle of the nineteenth century engineers and scientists understood that in theory an internal combustion engine, in which flammable fuel exploded to directly power the drive train, was more efficient. Several daunting technical challenges stood in the way of putting this theory into practice, including controlling the explosion in a confined space, achieving the correct air-fuel mixture, and timing the ignition at just the right interval of the piston's stroke.

The first successful internal combustion engine dated back to 1859. A Belgian engineer, Etienne Lenoir, modified a steam engine by fueling it with a **volatile** (rapidly expanding and easily ignited) air and coal gas mix. He then ignited it with an electric spark, so that the exhaust gases drove a **piston**. Lenoir's engine produced one horsepower and could power a water pump.

Three years later a French engineer, Alfonse Beau de Rochas, devised a more powerful and practical machine called a four-stroke engine. The four strokes worked as follows: The first

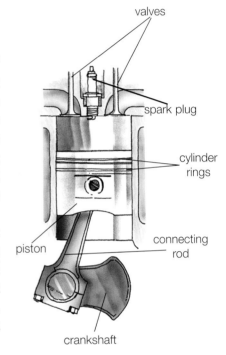

Below: A piston and cylinder. The piston rings insure a tight fit in the bore. Valves at the top allow a fuel mixture in and exhaust gases out. The spark plug produces an electric spark. A connecting rod links the piston and the crankshaft.

valves

spark plug

cylinder rings

piston

connecting rod

crankshaft

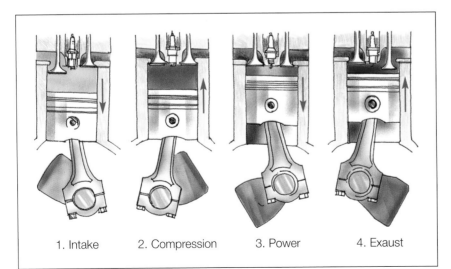

1. Intake   2. Compression   3. Power   4. Exaust

Left: A simplified cutaway of a four-stroke cycle of a gasoline engine—intake, compression, power, and exaust— showing the operating sequence of the valves and the movements of the piston. the cycle is repeated over and over again in each cylinder as the engine turns.

VOLATILE: rapidly evaporating and easy to ignite

PISTON: a disk or short rod made to closely fit in an engine cylinder so that changes in pressure inside the cylinder cause the piston to move. The motion of the piston is then used to drive machinery, such as the paddle wheel on a steamboat or the wheels of a locomotive.

The Daimler automobile of 1886 had four-seat accommodation with two persons on the higher bench seat forward of the engine and two more on the lower seat to the rear of the engine. A belt drive was used to power the rear wheels, and the front wheels were steered by a vertical shaft with four handles.

stroke (upward) drew the fuel mixture into the cylinder; the second (downward) stroke compressed it; when the compressed fuel was ignited, the ignition caused the third stroke, which provided power; and the fourth stroke exhausted the spent gases from the cylinder.

Not until 1876 did the German inventor Nikolaus Otto produce the first practical gas engine. Otto's so-called "silent engine" offered important advantages compared with steam engines. It could be fired up only when needed and could be run efficiently at a partial load. The fuel it required often derived from other industrial processes such as coking and smelting. The only disadvantage was its lack of mobility because it had to be connected to a source of gas.

Other German engineers worked with Otto's design. In 1885 Carl Benz (the "Benz" in the name "Mercedes Benz") made a self-propelled vehicle powered by a single-cylinder gasoline engine with electric ignition. The next year Gottlieb Daimler (the "Daimler" in "Daimler Chrysler") and Wilhelm Maybach invented the carburetor, a device that efficiently mixed fuel and air.

While these engineers were exploring internal combustion along one line of investigation, another German engineer, Rudolf Diesel, pursued a different approach. Diesel's starting point was the knowledge that compressing air raises its temperature. Diesel used that principal to eliminate the need for a spark to ignite the air-fuel mix. His invention squirted fuel into a cylinder of pressurized air at 800 degrees Celsius. At that temperature the fuel spontaneously ignited. The diesel engine used a cheaper, less flammable fuel and was more efficient because combustion occurred inside a smaller cylinder that produced twice the compression of a gasoline engine.

The first years of the new century saw the rise of petroleum and a new transportation revolution based on the mobile internal combustion engine. The development of the internal combustion engine broke the shackles that had tied engines to their fuel sources. A vehicle could carry its own liquid fuel supply, such as gasoline, and thus achieve convenient self-propulsion.

THE HORSELESS CARRIAGE

The first horseless carriages, or automobiles, were developed in Europe during the early 1890s. They used either steam or electric engines. The horseless carriage was a

Creative tinkerers and inventors worked to improve the newfangled horseless carriage. This heavy and awkward steam automobile was built in 1878.

A 1900 electric "horseless carriage."

popular novelty item among the French, German, and British upper class, who enjoyed displaying their wealth. However, the steam-propelled horseless carriage was both expensive and inconvenient because the vehicle had to carry a large volume of water, which added a lot of weight, and it took a long time to heat the water before it could begin moving. The electric horseless carriage, on the other hand, carried huge batteries that needed frequent recharging, and thus it lacked driving range.

THE AUTOMOBILE

In 1893 a pair of brothers, Charles and J. Frank Duryea, copied a published description of Benz's automobile and built a running model with a one-cylinder, two-cycle engine. Within 12 months they produced a second, more technically sophisticated two-cylinder, four-cycle vehicle. The Duryea brothers were just two among many inventors working on automobiles.

Their opportunity came when a Chicago newspaper sponsored an automobile race on Thanksgiving Day 1895. The Duryea automobile, driven by J. Frank Duryea, completed the 55-mile snow-covered course at an average speed of eight miles per hour and won the race. The victory brought valuable public attention. The brothers followed up their victory by producing a vehicle possessing several features that became standard on later vehicles, including a four-speed gear shift, water-cooled four-cylinder engine, and electric ignition.

Opposite: The development of the British automobile was almost fatally slowed by legislation that up to 1896 demanded that any motor vehicle on the public road system had to be preceded by a man with a red flag (day) or red lantern (night).

Also in 1895 a trade journal devoted to the automobile industry, *Horseless Age*, began publication. The editors determined that in the United States alone about 300 companies or individuals were building and testing experimental cars. Among them were the Duryea brothers, who founded their own automobile manufacturing company and sold their first model in 1896. The editors of the *Horseless Age* explained that "All over the country mechanics and inventors are wrestling with the problems" of manufacturing automobiles. Regarding the automobile's future, the journal claimed that "the growing needs of our civilization demand it [the automobile]; the public believe in it, and await with lively interest its practical application to the daily business of the world."

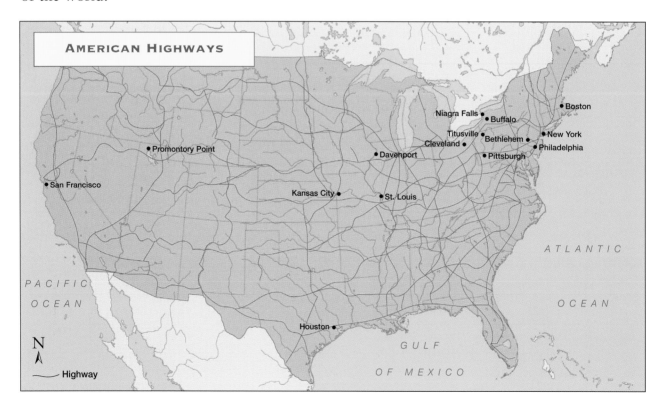

Henry Ford brought the automobile industry into the modern age. Ford's Model T, introduced in 1909, delivered an affordable automobile to the general public and created "a car culture" in the United States. Millions of Americans purchased new cars.

Just as the railroad era had caused tremendous expansion in related industries, so the expansion of the automobile industry led to growth in steel, glass, rubber, paint, leather, and most especially, petroleum production. Car owners wanted better roads, and that led to a satellite boom in road construction, automobile service stations, motels, fast food restaurants, and destination resorts. Within decades of the automobile's introduction America's social and cultural life underwent fundamental change.

HENRY FORD

Henry Ford was born in 1863 near Dearborn, Michigan. He dropped out of school to work as an apprentice machinist and

Opposite top: The Duryea brothers' 1893 gasoline-powered auto.

Opposite bottom: The development and spread of automobiles led to a boom in highway construction. By 1921 nearly 13,000 miles of federal highway had been built. Some 3.1 million miles of state and local roads covered the country, and 387,000 miles of them were paved.

Right: This humble workshop was the birthplace of the Ford Model T, perhaps the most important automobile that the world had ever seen.

Below: Henry Ford's first automobile, a demonstration gasoline model that he built in 1896.

quickly demonstrated his mechanical skills. He later worked in Detroit as chief engineer for the Edison Illuminating Company. Although poorly educated, Ford had the foresight to imagine that the future of transportation would rely on the automobile. Ford was a brilliant tinkerer and in 1896 built a demonstration car powered by an internal combustion engine. That led to a job working for the Detroit Automobile Company during which time he built his first race car.

In 1903 he founded the Ford Motor Company to manufacture affordable automobiles. He predicted that he would "build a motor car for the great multitude. It will be large enough for the family but small enough for the individual to run and care for. It will be constructed of the best materials, by the best men to be hired, after the simplest designs that modern engineering can devise."

Left: Henry Ford envisioned an America in which consumers would purchase ever more automobiles.

Below: Bodywork being attached to Ford Model T's on the assembly line.

Ford Model T's coming off a 1917 assembly line. By 1925 the Ford assembly line completed a car every ten seconds. By 1927 the automobile industry employed seven percent of all manufacturing workers and had stimulated a tremendous expansion of related industries.

Ford's vision came true in 1909 when his company built the Model T. On release the Model T cost $950; but as the company improved its assembly line, its sales volumes increased, and the price dropped. Ford had said that the Model T would be so low in price that no man making a good salary would be unable to own one. In 1919 about 10 percent of American families owned a car. By 1927 four out of five families owned cars. Ford's prediction had come true.

It took time for drivers in the early days of the automobile to learn that cars could not go everywhere that horses went.

The manufacturing innovations that Ford introduced forever changed the workplace. He created an efficient assembly line. As he described it, "Every piece of work in the shop moves" by hooks, overhead chains, powered platforms, or even gravity. Assembly-line production led to significant cost savings by making it possible to replace skilled workers with lower-cost unskilled laborers. Although the assembly line work was tedious, Ford paid his workers well and reduced their work week. He was the first employer to establish the weekend as free time, explaining that he wanted working families to "enjoy the blessings of pleasure in God's great open spaces" and to experience that pleasure by traveling in the automobile.

The vast increase in car ownership that Ford purposefully set out to accomplish changed American society. Ford influenced both daily life and manufacturing. From 1920 on, the manufacture of inexpensive goods by assembly-line production spread throughout industry.

This splendid 1909 Model T touring car was listed at $850.

THE ELECTRICITY NETWORK

Tinkerers and trained scientists had been investigating the nature of electricity since the middle of the eighteenth century. Scientists had learned that under certain conditions electricity produced light. They developed batteries that generated a continuous flow of electricity, but these batteries failed to produce enough current for illumination.

A key technical breakthrough occurred in 1831 when the British researcher Michael Faraday built an electric generator. Faraday's generator employed the principle of electromagnetic induction (whereby the opening and closing of an electric circuit caused a magnetic field around an electromagnet to grow and collapse, and cause, or induce, an electric current in a nearby but separate conductor). Unlike existing batteries, Faraday's generator produced a current strong enough to be used for lighting. Faraday's work soon led to arc lights in which electricity sparked across a gap between conducting wires to produce light.

Benjamin Franklin was among many whose experiments expanded scientific knowledge about electricity.

A REVOLUTION IN COMMUNICATIONS

Along with an efficient transportation system a fast and reliable communication system was necessary to sustain the later phases of the Industrial Revolution. The telegraph system had provided part of the solution. When the Scottish immigrant Alexander Graham Bell patented the telephone, a new age of instantaneous voice communication began.

THE TELEPHONE SYSTEM

Bell's father was an inventor and a speech teacher who had developed a form of sign language for teaching the deaf. His son followed in his footsteps. While working as a professor of vocal physiology at Boston University, Bell invented two key devices that together made possible the electrical transmission of speech. Basically, Bell's inventions converted electronic telegraph impulses into voice using very sensitive diaphragms. In 1876 Bell applied for a patent on his invention, the magnetoelectric telephone.

He knew from the experience of Samuel Morse, the inventor of the telegraph, that it was one thing to patent an invention and quite another to profit from it. Since he recognized that he had no particular skill at business, Bell founded a company to conduct the financial and administrative sides of creating a national telephone network.

Bell had 16 years of monopoly rights granted by his patent. During those years the businessmen and attorneys who managed the Bell Telephone Company worked successfully to build the company into a dominant position. They made the crucial decision to manufacture all the telephone instruments but to lease them to local companies that would actually operate the telephone exchanges. Under the terms of the lease Bell's company specified common technologies. In that way the company managed to standardize all telephones, telephone lines, and telephone exchanges. Because everything was standardized, long-distance service involving a series of local companies was possible.

The Bell Telephone Company expected its most important customers to be businesses. However, because businessmen wanted a written record of transactions, they continued to rely on mail and telegraph for most of their communications. Nonetheless, the company enjoyed explosive growth: After one year of operation it had leased 3,000 telephones; by 1880 there were 60,000; and in 1893, the year the patent ended, there were 260,000. About two-thirds of the lines were located in businesses. Certain businesses such as physicians and hospitals, lawyers, and liquor stores found the telephone particularly useful.

In 1885 the company reorganized into the American Telephone & Telegraph Company (AT&T). The men who ran the company had always expected that consumers would use the telephone as they used the telegraph, and therefore most consumers would be businessmen. They did not foresee the social implications of the new device. While telegraphic communication required intermediaries (telegraph operators), telephones allowed direct, person-to-person communication. Furthermore, voice communication facilitated emotional communication. Customers could use the telephone to socialize with one another, and they did. After the Bell patent ended, independent telephone companies gave consumers the choices they wanted, including dial telephones in their homes, and a social revolution began.

The telephone revolutionized communications. It became an essential tool for business and a common feature of the home. Alexander Graham Bell at the 1892 opening of the New York-Chicago telephone line.

European technicians developed the first practical electric generators (called dynamos) during the 1870s. The American inventor Charles Brush combined generators with arc lighting to develop a system in which generators produced electricity from a central station and transmitted it to widespread locations. At that time gas lamps provided street lighting. Brush believed that electric arc lighting was a superior technology. Brush overcame numerous technical challenges with a series of inventions such as high-voltage dynamos and automatic short circuits (to preserve the rest of a system when a light burned out). He built the nation's first arc lighting system for San Francisco's street lights in 1879 and the next year did the same in New York City, Philadelphia, and Boston.

In 1831 Michael Faraday built an electric generator that could create a continuous flow of current sufficient to be used for lighting.

A great deal of the electrical energy of an arc light was wasted in the generation of heat. In addition, arc lighting was too bright for indoor use. Accordingly, by the middle of the 1870s scientists were competing to develop a bulb in which electric light came from the glow of a highly resistant filament, or wire, instead of a spark across a gap between wires. To work efficiently, such a filament had to be kept in a vacuum. The American inventor Thomas Edison won the race to produce the first practical incandescent light bulb.

By the 1860s British and French lighthouses used giant arc lamps based on Faraday's research into electromagnetic induction. The technology soon spread to American lighthouses.

An early dynamo for the generation of alternating current, which was an improvement over direct current.

THOMAS EDISON

Thomas Edison was born in Ohio in 1847. His elementary school teachers thought he was a slow learner, so his parents took him from school and taught him at home. As a teenager Edison went car to car aboard trains selling newspapers, toiletries, and candy. He encountered telegraph operators and became interested in electricity. By 1863 he worked as a telegraph operator.

At a young age Edison displayed an interest in and talent for devising better ways to accomplish ordinary tasks. By 1869 he had invented his first patentable device, an electrographic vote recorder. He and a business partner cofounded an electrical engineering firm in New York, but a competitor soon bought them out. Edison used his profits to start a business entirely devoted to inventing new products.

His decision led to the construction of the famous office and research laboratory at Menlo Park, New Jersey, and later a larger lab in West Orange. Edison's research labs produced two historic inventions that changed people's everyday lives. In 1877 Edison invented the phonograph, which allowed people to listen to music and voice communications conveniently while at home. Two years later he developed the first practical incandescent light bulb. Henceforth there was no need to illuminate indoor spaces with fuel-burning lamps and candles.

While the phonograph and light bulb changed the way people lived, Edison's invention of an improved electric dynamo had even greater

Opposite: Thomas Edison was both an inventor and entrepreneur. He invented a feasible electric light, then created a system to deliver electricity to consumers, and founded companies to manufacture parts to build this system and provide the service. He also invented a phonograph, shown here, for playing sound recordings.

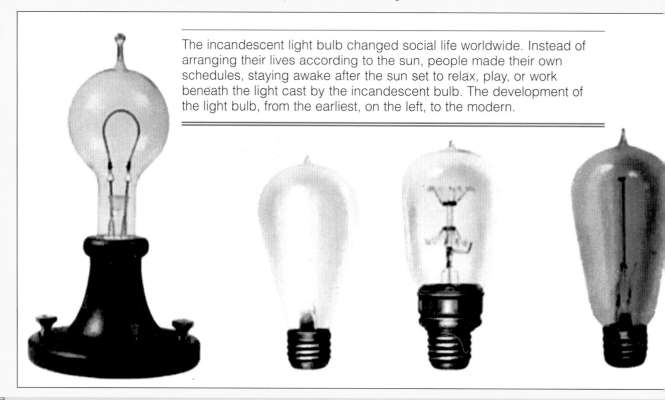

The incandescent light bulb changed social life worldwide. Instead of arranging their lives according to the sun, people made their own schedules, staying awake after the sun set to relax, play, or work beneath the light cast by the incandescent bulb. The development of the light bulb, from the earliest, on the left, to the modern.

industrial consequences. In combination with steam turbines, introduced during the 1890s, electricity could be generated practically everywhere. This capability promoted mass production in the manufacturing industries. In 1892 Edison merged his businesses to form General Electric for the purpose of developing alternating current products.

Many historians consider Edison to be America's greatest inventor. Not only did he create significant inventions, but he was the first person to make inventing itself a business. Because of the success of his research labs corporations then and thereafter made research and development important parts of their businesses.

Opposite top: New York City at night, fifty years after Edison Electric began lighting the city.

Opposite bottom: Nikola Tesla is said to have arrived in America with only four cents in his pocket. He first worked for Thomas Edison, but the two men did not get along, and he ended up working for Edison's competitor, George Westinghouse.

The dynamo (generator) room at the Edison Electric Lighting Station in New York City.

In addition to being a brilliant inventor, Edison was a shrewd businessman who understood how to develop both a new technology and a set of businesses to manage the technology. He founded the Edison Electric Light Company to develop the incandescent light bulb. In 1880 he established the Edison Electric Illuminating Company of New York to build and maintain the world's first central electrical generating station. Edison selected the station's site on Pearl Street for its location near Manhattan's highest concentration of office buildings, and he correctly supposed that these offices would become his customers. Edison had so successfully integrated his businesses that the Edison Machine Company built the station's generators, and the Edison Electric Tube Company manufactured the special underground cables that carried the electricity to the office buildings. Edison invented meters to measure the customers' electric usage. His employees installed lamp sockets that he had invented in the building, and of course, the bulbs used were his own.

The Edison Electric Illuminating Company of New York began operation in 1882. It was immediately successful. Within a few months entrepreneurs were applying to Edison

for licenses to build similar systems all around the world. Growth was so rapid that the United States went from one generating station in 1882 to 2,250 in 1902. The increasingly widespread availability of electricity led to a host of new electric machines such as the electric fan, iron, and vacuum cleaner.

Although Edison was arguably the foremost American inventor in history, during that era many other inventors and scientists made important contributions. The Serbian immigrant Nikola Tesla invented an alternating current motor in 1888. Tesla's invention caused a rapid increase in the industrial use of electrical motors. In 1894 a cotton mill became the first factory ever built that relied entirely on electric power. Simultaneously, existing factories began the conversion from steam power to electric power.

Direct current could be transmitted by wires only for short distances up to a few miles. A brilliant inventor, George Westinghouse, tackled the challenge of overcoming that limitation by improving alternating current electricity. He founded the Westinghouse Electric Company in 1884 to accomplish his goal and hired Tesla to help him. Although Westinghouse's efforts put him in competition with the formidable Edison companies (which dominated the direct current market), he pressed ahead. By 1892 Westinghouse had installed more than 1,000 alternating current systems for incandescent lighting. In 1895 he built the world's first generating plant designed to transmit power over longer distances—a hydroelectric plant at Niagara Falls that transmitted alternating current some 20 miles to consumers in Buffalo, New York. The large-scale generation of electricity and ability to send it long distances created immense new opportunities for using electric power.

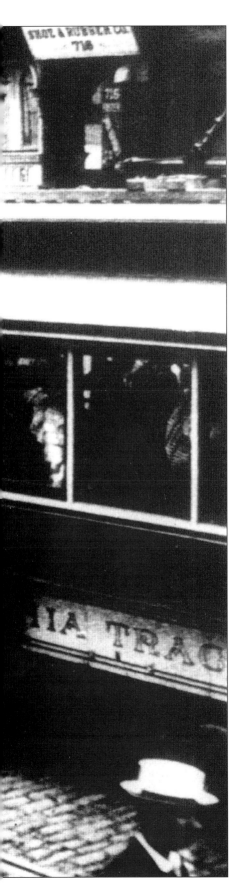

By 1910 electric-generating companies had become standardized, generating alternating current (Edison's system had generated direct current) at 60 cycles per minute. Standardization meant that power plants throughout the country could be linked into one vast network, while individual electric appliances could be manufactured to uniform specifications. Generating companies became known as "utility" companies. Utility means the property of being useful. Industry and private consumers had found electricity to be so useful that it played a constantly expanding role in almost all aspects of life.

Left: In 1880 some 100,000 horses hauled 19,000 urban streetcars. Eight years later came the first electric streetcar system and the rapid replacement of horsepower by electrical power. Frank Sprague, an electrical engineer, designed and built the first electric streetcar system in Richmond, Virginia, in 1888. Fourteen years later there were 22,576 miles of streetcar track in America. By 1903, 98 percent of all streetcars ran by electricity. A Philadelphia street in 1897, shared by electric trolleys and horse-drawn wagons.

Above: George Westinghouse and his Westinghouse Electric Company dominated the alternating current electric-generating market.

ANDREW CARNEGIE AND AMERICA'S AGE OF STEEL

Above: When Andrew Carnegie sold his company in 1901, the financier J.P. Morgan sent his congratulations for "just having become the richest man in the world."

Opposite: Bessemer steel was ideal for manufacturing railroad tracks. In 1873 U.S. producers made about 800,000 tons of iron rails, compared to 115,000 tons of Bessemer steel rails. After that Bessemer production increased to dominate this market. Making Bessemer steel in Pittsburgh in 1886.

Andrew Carnegie was born in Scotland in 1835, the son of a handloom weaver. The widespread adoption of power looms forced his family to emigrate to the United States to find work. As a young teenager, Carnegie worked long hours in a cotton factory earning $1.20 per week. He soon concluded that in order to advance in life, he needed an education, so he began night school.

In 1850, at age 15, he left the factory to work as a messenger boy in a Pittsburgh telegraph office. He worked hard and impressed his employers while continuing his night schooling. The superintendent of the Pennsylvania Railroad hired him as his personal clerk and telegraph operator. The superintendent recognized Carnegie's value and promoted him. Simultaneously, the young man started carefully investing in selected industries and began building his fortune. Within five years of his first investment of $217 he was earning $5,000 in dividends alone.

In 1865 Carnegie resigned from the Pennsylvania Railroad and invested in a Pittsburgh ironworks. He traveled widely to learn about new iron and steel technologies, and applied what he had learned to his Pittsburgh business. A combination of strict cost cutting and aggressive marketing saw his business prosper.

Five years later Carnegie expanded his business to include pig iron production (vertical integration in which a company replaces its suppliers by assuming their duties). A deep American economic downturn allowed Carnegie to buy up bankrupt iron and steel companies at very low prices. He built a new steel mill that utilized the most recent technology, including the Bessemer process (see Volume 7). Its 10 converters produced high-grade steel at significantly lower cost than competitors. By 1877 his mill produced 15 percent of all U.S. Bessemer steel.

Carnegie continued the process of vertical integration by acquiring a coal and coke company and later by leasing large plots of iron-rich land in Minnesota. The ore moved across the Great Lakes aboard Carnegie steamships and traveled to his mills along rail lines he owned. So complete was his vertical integration that by 1899, the year he incorporated the Carnegie Steel Company, Andrew Carnegie virtually controlled the country's entire steel industry.

During that period, one of Carnegie's leading business partners ruthlessly broke the strike at his factory in Homestead, Pennsylvania, and his public reputation suffered. In 1901 he sold his interests in his company and became probably the richest man in the world, with a half a billion dollars in bonds from the sale. He spent the rest of his life giving money to charitable causes. He expressed his vision in a book, *The Gospel of Wealth*, where he explained that the rich should redistribute their wealth rather than merely leaving it to their offspring.

Carnegie was a complex character, a man who relentlessly cut costs and exploited labor to increase profits and then gave his money away to fund projects for world peace, higher education, library construction, and scientific research.

Some 800 employees of Carnegie Steel Works in Homestead, Pennsylvania, belonged to a steelworkers' union, which Andrew Carnegie decided to destroy. Carnegie's partner hired a private security force to patrol the factory, and then he cut wages, which goaded the employees to go on strike. An armed confrontation erupted between the strikers and the security force, killing a dozen men. The state governor called out the militia. The strikers finally gave in after five months, and work resumed at longer hours and lower pay. Although many viewed the strikers as dangerous radicals, Carnegie Steel's ruthlessness did not escape public notice.

THE GROWTH OF THE U.S. STEEL INDUSTRY

The British inventor Henry Bessemer had perfected a new method of steel production in 1856. Eight years later the first Bessemer forge in the United States opened in Troy, New York. The passage of four more years saw the introduction of the open hearth process (or Siemens-Martin process, see Volume 7). These developments enabled the mass production of steel.

The railroads drove demand for Bessemer steel. They preferred it because it was more durable than either conventional steel or softer iron rails. The Bethlehem Steel Company in Pennsylvania, founded in 1873, was the first American company to mass-produce Bessemer steel.

Seven years earlier, in 1866, U.S. government surveyors had discovered the largest known deposit of iron ore in the world, in the Mesabi Range of northern Minnesota. Here was high-quality ore that was conveniently located near Lake Superior. By 1873 barges cheaply transported more than one million tons of ore each year to mills in Indiana, Ohio, and Pennsylvania. The Mesabi Range was a key factor allowing American producers to make high-quality, low-cost iron and steel, and thus outcompete foreign producers.

Above: Sir Henry Bessemer's skill as an inventor brought him varied honors. He was knighted in 1879, and in 1887 a steelmaking town in Alabama was named after him.

Below: Developed in Europe during the late 1800s, the open hearth furnace represented a great advance over previous methods of heating iron, making possible the production of higher-quality steel. Open hearth furnaces used the waste gases generated during the heating of the pig iron to warm a honeycomb of bricks. The bricks, in turn, superheated the air and gas to achieve a far higher furnace temperature, which made it possible to remove more impurities from iron. An open hearth furnace at an Illinois steel plant around 1899.

STEEL-MAKING FACILITIES

The ability to mine iron ore, transport it, and turn it into useful objects advanced dramatically through more than 300 years of American history. Iron mining had once relied entirely on men using picks and shovels. By 1900 powerful digging machines assisted American miners (left, in the Mesabi Range, Minnesota). Rail cars and barges delivered the iron ore for processing at steel plants (below, a plant near Pittsburgh, Pennsylvania). During the 1640s in a colonial Massachusetts iron works (far left), human power alone hammered iron into shape or poured it into molds. By the 1890s great furnaces heated iron, turned it into steel, and shaped the steel for its ultimate use. The rolling mill (far lower left) and press shop and furnaces (lower left) at Homestead Steel Works in Pennsylvania

Main picture: The Mesabi range in Minnesota yielded a valuable type of iron ore. Iron ore barges at the Lake Superior docks of Duluth, Minnesota, 1903

Right: Bessemer steel provided the structural integrity to build tall urban buildings, the so-called "skyscrapers," Erecting the Empire State Building in 1930.

With Carnegie's mills leading the way, by the early 1890s total U.S. iron and steel production exceeded that of Great Britain. It was a historic moment, symbolic of the American climb to the top of the industrial world. The United States produced almost half of the world's supply of steel ingots in 1895. Its lead increased such that by 1915 America produced over three times more pig iron than Great Britain.

Steel:
See also
Volume 7 pages 53–56

CONCLUSION

The second phase of the American Industrial Revolution transformed the nation. In 1869 agriculture had contributed 53 percent of total American production and manufacturing 33 percent. After just 30 years the numbers reversed, with manufacturing accounting for over half of all production and agriculture just one-third.

A DATELINE OF MAJOR EVENTS DURING THE INDUSTRIAL REVOLUTION

BEFORE 1750	1760	1770	1780

REVOLUTIONS IN INDUSTRY AND TECHNOLOGY

1619: English settlers establish the first iron works in colonial America, near Jamestown, Virginia.

1689: Thomas Savery (England) patents the first design for a steam engine.

1709: Englishman Abraham Darby uses coke instead of coal to fuel his blast furnace.

1712: Englishman Thomas Newcomen builds the first working steam engine.

1717: Thomas Lombe establishes a silk-throwing factory in England.

1720: The first Newcomen steam engine on the Continent is installed at a Belgian coal mine.

1733: James Kay (England) invents the flying shuttle.

1742: Benjamin Huntsman begins making crucible steel in England.

1756: The first American coal mine opens.

1764: In England James Hargreaves invents the spinning jenny.

1769: Englishman Richard Arkwright patents his spinning machine, called a water frame.

James Watt of Scotland patents an improved steam engine design.

Josiah Wedgwood (England) opens his Etruria pottery works.

1771: An industrial spy smuggles drawings of the spinning jenny from England to France.

1774: John Wilkinson (England) builds machines for boring cannon cylinders.

1775: Arkwright patents carding, drawing, and roving machines.

In an attempt to end dependence on British textiles American revolutionaries open a spinning mill in Philadelphia using a smuggled spinning-jenny design.

1777: Oliver Evans (U.S.) invents a card-making machine.

1778: John Smeaton (England) introduces cast iron gearing to transfer power from waterwheels to machinery.

The water closet (indoor toilet) is invented in England.

1779: Englishman Samuel Crompton develops the spinning mule.

1783: Englishman Thomas Bell invents a copper cylinder to print patterns on fabrics.

1784: Englishman Henry Cort invents improved rollers for rolling mills and the puddling process for refining pig iron.

Frenchman Claude Berthollet discovers that chlorine can be used as a bleach.

The ironworks at Le Creusot use France's first rotary steam engine to power its hammers, as well as using the Continent's first coke-fired blast furnace.

1785: Englishman Edmund Cartwright invents the power loom.

1788: The first steam engine is imported into Germany.

REVOLUTIONS IN TRANSPORTATION AND COMMUNICATION

1757: The first canal is built in England.

Locks on an English canal

1785: The first canal is built in the United States, at Richmond, Virginia.

1787: John Fitch and James Rumsey (U.S.) each succeed in launching a working steamboat.

SOCIAL REVOLUTIONS

1723: Britain passes an act to allow the establishment of workhouses for the poor.

1750: The enclosure of common land gains momentum in Britain.

1776: Scottish professor Adam Smith publishes *The Wealth of Nations*, which promotes laissez-faire capitalism.

The workhouse

INTERNATIONAL RELATIONS

Continental Army in winter quarters at Valley Forge

1775 –1783: The American Revolution. Thirteen colonies win their independence from Great Britain and form a new nation, the United States of America.

1789–1793: The French Revolution leads to abolition of the monarchy and execution of the king and queen. Mass executions follow during the Reign of Terror, 1793–1794.

1790 | **1800** | **1810** | **1820**

1790: English textile producer Samuel Slater begins setting up America's first successful textile factory in Pawtucket, Rhode Island.

Jacob Perkins (U.S.) invents a machine capable of mass-producing nails.

1791: French chemist Nicholas Leblanc invents a soda-making process.

1793: Eli Whitney (U.S.) invents a cotton gin.

1794: Germany's first coke-fired blast furnace is built.

The first German cotton spinning mill installs Arkwright's water frame.

1798: Eli Whitney devises a system for using power-driven machinery to produce interchangeable parts, the model for the "American System" of manufacture.

Wool-spinning mills are built in Belgium using machinery smuggled out of England.

A cylindrical papermaking machine is invented in England.

1801: American inventor Oliver Evans builds the first working high-pressure steam engine and uses it to power a mill.

Joseph-Marie Jacquard (France) invents a loom that uses punch cards to produce patterned fabrics.

A cotton-spinning factory based on British machinery opens in Belgium.

The first cotton-spinning mill in Switzerland begins operation.

Austria establishes the Continent's largest cotton-spinning mill.

1802: In England William Murdock uses coal gas to light an entire factory.

Richard Trevithick builds a high-pressure steam engine in England.

1807: British businessmen open an industrial complex in Belgium that includes machine manufacture, coal mining, and iron production.

1808: Russia's first spinning mill begins production in Moscow.

1810: Henry Maudslay (England) invents the precision lathe.

1816: Steam power is used for the first time in an American paper mill.

English scientist Humphry Davy invents a safety lamp for coal miners in England.

1817: The French iron industry's first puddling works and rolling mills are established.

1819: Thomas Blanchard (U.S.) invents a gunstock-turning lathe, which permits production of standardized parts.

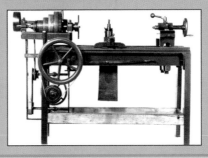

A turning lathe

1821: Massachusetts businessmen begin developing Lowell as a site for textile mills.

1822: Power looms are introduced in French factories.

1820s: Spinning mills begin operation in Sweden.

Steam power is first used in Czech industry.

1827: A water-driven turbine is invented in France.

1794: The 66-mile Philadelphia and Lancaster turnpike begins operation.

Along an American Highway

1802: In England Richard Trevithick builds his first steam locomotive.

1807: Robert Fulton launches the Clermont, the first commercially successful steamboat, on the Hudson River in New York.

1811: Robert Fulton and his partner launch the first steamboat on the Mississippi River.

Construction begins on the Cumberland Road (later renamed the National Road) from Baltimore, Maryland, to Wheeling, Virginia.

1815: In England John McAdam develops an improved technique for surfacing roads.

1819: The first steamship crosses the Atlantic Ocean.

1825: The 363-mile Erie Canal is completed in America.

In England the first passenger railroad, the Stockton and Darlington Railway, begins operation.

1826: The 2-mile horse-drawn Granite Railroad in Massachusetts becomes the first American railroad.

1790: First American patent law passed.

Philadelphia begins building a public water system.

1798: Robert Owen takes over the New Lanark mills and begins implementing his progressive ideas.

1800: Parliament prohibits most labor union activity.

1802: Parliament passes a law limiting the working hours of poor children and orphans.

1811–1816: Luddite rioters destroy textile machinery in England.

1819: Parliament extends legal protection to all child laborers.

British cavalry fire at demonstrators demanding voting reform in Manchester, killing 11 and wounding hundreds, including women and children.

1827: Carpenters organize the first national trade union in Britain.

18th–century carpenter

1799: Napoleon Bonaparte seizes control of France's government.

1792–1815: The Napoleonic Wars involve most of Europe, Great Britain, and Russia. France occupies many of its neighboring nations, reorganizes their governments, and changes their borders.

1812–1815: War between the United States and Great Britain disrupts America's foreign trade and spurs the development of American industry.

61

A DATELINE OF MAJOR EVENTS DURING THE INDUSTRIAL REVOLUTION

	1830	1840	1850	1860
REVOLUTIONS IN INDUSTRY AND TECHNOLOGY	**1830:** Switzerland's first weaving mill established. **1831:** British researcher Michael Faraday builds an electric generator. American inventor Cyrus McCormick builds a horse-drawn mechanical reaper. **1834:** Bulgaria's first textile factory is built. **1835:** Samuel Colt (U.S) invents the Colt revolver. The first steam engine is used to power a paper mill in Croatia. **1836:** The first Hungarian steam mill, the Pest Rolling Mill company, begins using steam power to process grain. **1837:** The first successful coke-fired blast furnace in the United States begins operation.	American blacksmith John Deere introduces the first steel plow. **1842:** Britain lifts restrictions on exporting textile machinery.  Making Bessemer steel	**1849:** The California Gold Rush begins. **1850:** Swedish sawmills begin using steam power. **1851:** The Great Exhibition opens at the Crystal Palace in London. William Kelly of Kentucky invents a process for converting pig iron to steel. **1852:** Hydraulic mining is introduced in the American West. **1853:** The first cotton-spinning mill opens in India. **1856:** William Perkin (England) synthesizes the first coal tar dye. Henry Bessemer (England) announces his process for converting pig iron to steel. Isaac Singer (U.S.) introduces the sewing machine.	**1859:** Edwin Drake successfully drills for oil in Pennsylvania. **1863:** Ernest Solvay of Belgium begins working on a process to recover ammonia from soda ash in order to produce bleaching powder. **1864:** Switzerland's first major chemical company is established. The Siemens-Martin open-hearth steelmaking process is perfected in France. **1865:** The first oil pipeline opens in America. The rotary web press is invented in America, permitting printing on both sides of the paper. **1866:** U.S. government surveyors discover the largest-known deposit of iron ore in the world in the Mesabi Range of northern Minnesota.
REVOLUTIONS IN TRANSPORTATION AND COMMUNICATION	**1830:** The first locomotive-powered railroad to offer regular service begins operating in South Carolina. The opening of the Liverpool and Manchester Railway marks the beginning of the British railroad boom. **1833:** The 60-mile Camden and Amboy Railroad of New Jersey is completed. **1835:** Construction begins on Germany's first railroad.	**1836:** First railroad built in Russia. **1843:** Tunnel completed under the Thames River, London, England, the world's first to be bored through soft clay under a riverbed. **1844:** Samuel Morse (U.S.) sends the first message via his invention, the telegraph. The nation's first steam-powered sawmill begins operation on the West Coast.	**1846:** First railroad built in Hungary. **1853:** The first railway is completed in India. **1854:** Americans complete the Moscow-St. Petersburg railroad line. **1855:** Switzerland's first railroad opens.	**1859:** In France Etienne Lenoir invents an internal combustion engine. **1860–1861:** The Pony Express, a system of relay riders, carries mail to and from America's West Coast. **1866:** The transatlantic telegraph cable is completed. Congress authorizes construction of a transcontinental telegraph line. **1869:** The tracks of two railroad companies meet at Promontory, Utah, to complete America's first transcontinental railroad
SOCIAL REVOLUTIONS	**1833:** Parliament passes the Factory Act to protect children working in textile factories. **1836–1842:** The English Chartist movement demands Parliamentary reform, but its petitions are rejected by Parliament. **1838:** The U.S. Congress passes a law regulating steamboat boiler safety, the first attempt by the federal government to regulate private behavior in the interest of public safety.	**1842:** Parliament bans the employment of children and women underground in mines. **1845:** Russia bans strikes. **1847:** A new British Factory Act limits working hours to 10 hours a day or 58 hours a week for children aged 13 to 18 and for women. **1848:** Marx and Engels coauthor the Communist Manifesto.	**1854:** In England Charles Dickens publishes *Hard Times*, a novel based on his childhood as a factory worker. **1857:** Brooklyn, New York, builds a city wastewater system.	**1860–1910:** More than 20 million Europeans emigrate to the United States. **1866:** National Labor Union forms in the United States. **1869:** Knights of Labor forms in the United States. Founding of the Great Atlantic and Pacific Tea Company (A&P) in the U.S.
INTERNATIONAL RELATIONS	**1839–1842:** Great Britain defeats China in a war and forces it to open several ports to trade.	**1847:** Austro-Hungary occupies Italy. **1848:** Failed revolutions take place in France, Germany, and Austro-Hungary. Serfdom ends in Austro-Hungary.	**1853:** The American naval officer Commodore Matthew Perry arrives in Japan. **1853–1856:** France, Britain, and Turkey defeat Russia in the Crimean War. **1858:** Great Britain takes control of India, retaining it until 1947.	**1861–1865:** The American Civil War brings about the end of slavery in the United States and disrupts raw cotton supplies for U.S. and foreign cotton mills. **1867:** Britain gains control of parts of Malaysia. Malaysia is a British colony from 1890 to 1957.

1870	1880	1890	1900

1860s: Agricultural machinery introduced in Hungary.

1870: John D. Rockefeller establishes the Standard Oil Company (U.S.).

1873: The Bethlehem Steel Company begins operation in Pennsylvania.

1875: The first modern iron and steel works opens in India.

Investment in the Japan's cotton industry booms.

1876: Philadelphia hosts the Centennial Exposition.

1877: Hungary installs its first electrical system.

1879: Charles Brush builds the nation's first arc-lighting system in San Francisco.

Thomas Edison (U.S.) develops the first practical incandescent light bulb.

1870s: Japan introduces mechanical silk-reeling.

1882: In New York City the Edison Electric Illuminating Company begins operating the world's first centralized electrical generating station.

1884: The U.S. Circuit Court bans hydraulic mining.

George Westinghouse (U.S.) founds Westinghouse Electric Company.

English engineer Charles Parsons develops a steam turbine.

1885: The introduction of band saws makes American lumbering more efficient.

German inventor Carl Benz builds a self-propelled vehicle powered by a single cylinder gas engine with electric ignition.

1887: An English power plant is the first to use steam turbines to generate electricity.

1888: Nikola Tesla (U.S.) invents an

alternating current electric motor.

1894: An American cotton mill becomes the first factory ever built to rely entirely on electric power.

1895: George Westinghouse builds the world's first generating plant designed to transmit power over longer distances—a hydroelectric plant at Niagara Falls to

transmit alternating current some 20 miles to consumers in Buffalo, New York.

1901: The United States Steel Corporation is formed by a merger of several American companies.

Japan opens its first major iron and steel works.

1929: The U.S.S.R. begins implementing its first Five-Year Plan, which places nationwide industrial development under central government control.

Power generators at Edison Electric

1875: Japan builds its first railway.

1876: In the U.S. Alexander Graham Bell invents the telephone.

German inventor Nikolaus Otto produces a practical gasoline engine.

1870s: Sweden's railroad boom.

1883: Brooklyn Bridge completed.

1885: Germans Gottlieb Daimler and Wilhelm Maybach build the world's first motorcycle.

1886: Daimler and Maybach invent the carburetor, the device that efficiently mixes fuel and air in internal combustion engines

1888: The first electric urban streetcar system begins operation in Richmond, Virginia.

1893: American brothers Charles and J. Frank Duryea build a working gasoline-powered automobile.

1896: Henry Ford builds a demonstration car powered by an internal combustion engine.

1896–1904: Russia builds the Manchurian railway in China.

1903: Henry Ford establishes Ford Motor Company.

1904: New York City subway system opens.

Trans-Siberian Railroad completed.

1908: William Durant, maker of horse-drawn carriages, forms the General Motors Company.

1909: Ford introduces the Model T automobile.

1870: Parliament passes a law to provide free schooling for poor children.

1872: France bans the International Working Men's Association.

1874: France applies its child labor laws to all industrial establishments and provides for inspectors to enforce the laws.

1877: Wage cuts set off the Great Railroad Strike in West Virginia, and the strike spreads across the country. Federal troops kill 35 strikers.

1880: Parliament makes school attendance compulsory for children between the ages of 5 and 10.

1881: India passes a factory law limiting child employment.

1884: Germany passes a law requiring employers to provide insurance against workplace accidents.

1886: American Federation of Labor forms.

1887: U.S. Interstate Commerce Act passed to regulate railroad freight charges.

1890: The U.S. government outlaws monopolies with passage of the Sherman Antitrust Act.

1892: Workers strike at Carnegie Steel in Homestead, Pennsylvania, in response to wage cuts. An armed confrontation results in 12 deaths.

1894: The Pullman strike, called in response to wage cuts, halts American railroad traffic. A confrontation with 2,000 federal troops kills 12 strikers in Chicago.

1900: Japan passes a law to limit union activity.

1902: The United Mine Workers calls a nationwide strike against coal mines, demanding eight-hour workdays and higher wages.

1903: Socialists organize the Russian Social Democratic Workers Party.

1931: Japan passes a law to limit working hours for women and children in textile factories.

1870: The city-states of Italy unify to form one nation.

1871: Parisians declare self-government in the city but are defeated by government forces.

Prussia and the other German states unify to form the German Empire.

1877–1878: War between Russia and Turkey. Bulgaria gains independence from Turkey.

1900–1901: A popular uprising supported by the Chinese government seeks to eject all foreigners from China.

1917: Russian Revolution

1929: A worldwide economic depression begins.

INDUSTRIALISTS AND INVENTORS

ALFONSE BEAU DE ROCHAS: 1815–1893; born in Monaco (between France and Italy). Beau de Rochas had the idea for a successful four-stroke engine and patented his concept in 1862, but he never built an operating model.

ALEXANDER GRAHAM BELL: 1847–1922; born in Scotland. Bell had only three years of formal education and graduated from a high school in Scotland at the age of 14. Bell's father trained him to carry on his work related to speech. The family moved to Canada for the sake of his health after his two brothers died. The parents of two of Bell's deaf students helped finance his work on developing a telephone. Bell had a wide variety of other interests and projects aside from the telephone. He also originated the idea for *National Geographic* magazine while serving as president of the National Geographic Society.

CARL BENZ: 1844–1929; born in Germany. Carl Benz designed and built the world's first gasoline-powered automobile, a three-wheeled car. His company went on to produce four-wheeled cars and racing cars. Benz merged his company with that of Gottlieb Daimler to form Daimler-Benz in 1926. The new company made Mercedes-Benz automobiles.

CHARLES BRUSH: 1849–1929; born in Ohio. Brush first applied his inventions to the project of lighting Wannamaker's, a Philadelphia department store, in 1878. He also installed streetlights in Cleveland, Ohio, before going on to light bigger cities. In addition to his electric company, he founded other manufacturing businesses.

ANDREW CARNEGIE: 1835–1919; born in Scotland. Andrew Carnegie's father was a hand-loom weaver who lost his livelihood to industrialization. The family emigrated to the United States and arrived at a town near Pittsburgh, Pennsylvania, in 1848. Through hard work, education, saving, careful investment, and innovative thinking Carnegie advanced from a teenage cotton mill employee to a major industrialist and possibly the wealthiest man of his era. After selling his steel company, he donated large sums to fund a university, a school for blacks, and pensions for workers. (See pages 52 and 54 of this volume for more about Carnegie.)

GOTTLIEB DAIMLER: 1834–1900; born in Germany. After first working for Nikolaus Otto, Daimler and Wilhelm Maybach left to start their own business building internal combustion engines. They designed a variety of automobiles, and in 1885 they added an engine to a bicycle, building the world's first motorcycle. Daimler and Maybach formed another business and began building Mercedes autos in 1899.

JOHN DEERE: 1804–1886; born in Vermont. Deere began working as an apprentice blacksmith while in his teens and eventually set up his own shop. After moving to prairie country in Illinois, he developed the steel plow. He founded his own farm equipment manufacturing company in 1868.

RUDOLF DIESEL: 1858–1913; born in Paris. Although born to German parents, Diesel grew up in France and England. In addition to working as an engineer, he took an interest in the arts and spoke several languages. His invention of the diesel engine made him a wealthy man. He is believed to have fallen overboard and drowned at sea while on the way to London.

EDWIN DRAKE: 1819–1880; born in New York State. Drake was a train conductor who owned a few shares of stock in the Pennsylvania Rock Oil Company, which operated near Titusville, Pennsylvania, obtaining oil from ground-level seeps. Drake traveled to Titusville and arranged to drill on company land, where he struck oil at 69 feet underground. Drake did not patent his drilling technique and never profited from his success. He fell into poverty, but the state of Pennsylvania gave him a pension in honor of his achievement.

DURYEA BROTHERS: Charles Duryea, 1861-1938, and James Frank Duryea, 1869-1967, were born in Illinois. The older Duryea brother, Charles, worked in the bicycle business and first had the idea for a gas-powered car after seeing a small gas engine at a state fair. He developed a car design by 1891 and with his brother built a working model by 1893. They manufactured 13 models of their car, but the business failed. The brothers later quarreled about who deserved the most credit for their first automobile. Separately, Charles went on to build three-wheeled cars, and Frank built luxury limousines.

THOMAS EDISON: 1847–1931; born in Ohio. Branded as a slow learner at school, Edison was probably just bored. At the age of 10 he set up a laboratory in his family's basement. Edison patented more than 1,000 inventions, including a movie projector. (See pages 46–48 of this volume for more about Edison).

MICHAEL FARADAY: 1791–1867; born in England. Son of a blacksmith and trained as a bookbinder, Faraday pursued his interest in science and attended lectures by the chemist Sir Humphrey Davy (see Volume 3). He became Davy's assistant and went on to become an engineer and chemist in his own right. In addition to his work in electrical generation, he was the first chemist to liquefy chlorine and isolate benzene.

HENRY FORD: 1863–1947; born in Michigan. The son of Irish immigrants, Henry Ford dropped out of school to become an apprentice machinist. He applied his impressive mechanical ability to the task of building a demonstration model of an automobile in 1896. In 1903 he established Ford Motor Company, which revolutionized American transportation by manufacturing affordable automobiles and revolutionized manufacturing by introducing the moving assembly line. Later in life Ford tried to enter politics by running for the U.S. Senate, but he was defeated. (See pages 37–40 of this volume for more about Ford.)

ETIENNE LENOIR: 1822–1900; born in Belgium. Some of the internal combustion engines that Lenoir built still ran smoothly after 20 years. More than a thousand were used in Britain and France to run various types of machinery. Lenoir built an automobile in 1862 and made a 6-mile, 2-hour trip in it. He also built a motorboat in 1886.

CYRUS MCCORMICK: 1809–1884; born in Virginia. McCormick's father, a farmer and inventor, had tried and failed to build a mechanical reaper. Cyrus had little formal education and spent long hours in his father's workshop. By the time he was 22 years old, he had designed a working horse-drawn reaper. The earliest model was so noisy that it frightened the horses that were pulling it. McCormick moved to Illinois so he could sell his reapers in the heart of farm country and founded the McCormick Harvesting Company. McCormick's company merged with several others in 1902 to form International Harvester, presided over by his son.

WILHELM MAYBACH: 1846–1929; born in Germany. In association with Gottlieb Daimler, Maybach built internal combustion engines and automobiles, including the Mercedes. In 1909 he founded a company that built aircraft engines. A brand of luxury automobile bears his name.

J.P. MORGAN: 1837–1913; born in Connecticut. Educated in America and Europe, John Pierpont Morgan worked for several banks, including one owned by his father. He formed his own finance company and arranged funding for major American industrial firms, including International Harvester, U.S. Steel, General Electric, and several railroads. His influence was so widespread throughout the business world that he drew criticism from journalists and social reformers.

ALFRED NOBEL: 1833–1896; born in Sweden. Descended from a scientist and an engineer, Nobel received his early education from tutors. By the age of 16 he spoke five languages and had a working knowledge of chemistry. He lived in Russia, France, and the United States while continuing his education. The explosion of his nitroglycerine factory brought him a reputation as a "mad scientist." His work with explosives and invention of dynamite earned him a huge fortune.

NIKOLAUS OTTO: 1832–1891; born in Germany. Otto built a gasoline-powered engine in 1861. In 1876 he was the first to build a four-stroke engine similar to the design patented by Alfonse Beau de Rochas. Otto built and sold at least 30,000 of these engines before he lost his patent in a legal conflict with Beau de Rochas.

JOHN D. ROCKEFELLER, SR.: 1839–1937, born in New York State. By the age of 20 he set up a business buying and selling hay, grain, and meats. When Congress passed the Sherman Antitrust Act in 1890, Rockefeller tried to get around the law by dissolving and reorganizing the trust that ran Standard Oil. Not until 1911 did Rockefeller finally have to break up the company. (See pages 30–31 of this volume for more about Rockefeller.)

ISAAC M. SINGER: 1811–1875; born in New York state. Singer went to work as an apprentice machinist at the age of 19. He invented a rock drill and a wood-carving machine. After repairing a customer's early-model sewing machine, Singer came up with a new design. Many features of Singer's design are still a standard part of modern sewing machines.

NIKOLA TESLA: 1856–1943, born in Croatia. Son of a Serbian Orthodox priest, Tesla attended universities and worked in laboratories throughout Europe before emigrating to the United States in 1884. In addition to his pioneering work with magnetic fields and alternating current, Tesla built a remote-control boat and worked on wireless power transmission. He drew ridicule for his belief that he was receiving communication from another planet and his claim to have invented a death ray, but such was his intuitive genius that modern scientists still comb his notes looking for inspiration. A unit of measurement related to magnetism is named after him.

GEORGE WESTINGHOUSE: 1846–1914; born in New York State. During the Civil War Westinghouse joined the Union Army at the age of 15 and later served in the Navy. After the war, he invented a steam engine, a water meter, an air brake for trains, and gas pipeline equipment. When Westinghouse introduced alternating current for electric power generation, it sparked a controversy among those who favored direct current. His chief competitor, Thomas Edison, arranged—over Westinghouse's objections—for New York State to use a Westinghouse alternating current generator to power the electric chair that executed condemned criminals. However, alternating current's superiority overcame the bad publicity.

GLOSSARY

ALTERNATING CURRENT: a type of electrical current that changes direction and so cycles between a specific peak power and zero. Alternating current (AC) was an improvement over direct current (DC) because it could more efficiently be transmitted over long distances.

ARC LAMP: a bright light in which electricity sparks across a gap between conducting wires. Arc lamps were used in lighthouses but were too bright for interior lighting

BAND SAW: a saw with a blade that forms a continuous band, mounted on pulleys

BOARD OF TRUSTEES: a group of trusted individuals who run a business on behalf of the shareholders

CAPITAL-INTENSIVE: requiring a lot of money

CARBURETOR: a device for mixing fuel and air in an internal combustion engine

CIRCULAR SAW: a saw in the form of a large metal disk with a toothed cutting edge

COMBINE: a piece of agricultural equipment that can perform several tasks at once

CONSERVATION: preserving natural resources from damage

CONTROLLING INTEREST: ownership of a majority of shares in a company, permitting the owner to run the business

CROSSCUT SAW: a long, narrow saw used to cut wood across the grain

DISTILL: to purify a material by boiling and then cooling it, so that it condenses into a new container, leaving the impurities behind in the old container; to separate mixtures into their individual components

DREDGE: to widen or deepen a waterway by removing silt

DYNAMO: electric power generator

ECONOMIES OF SCALE: savings realized by operating big plants or businesses

ELECTROMAGNETIC: generating a current by opening and closing an electrical circuit to cause a magnetic field to grow and collapse

FLUME: a ditch or trough that carries water down a mountainside; similar to a sluice

HOLDING COMPANY: a company that owns other companies

HORSEPOWER: a unit of engine power believed to be equivalent to the power of a horse

HYDRAULIC MINING: extracting minerals from soil by shooting a jet of water at the soil and washing it into sluices

HYDROELECTRIC: using flowing water to generate electricity

INCANDESCENT: heated by electric current to the point at which it glows, producing light. Incandescent lights were better suited to interior lighting than arc lamps, which were too bright.

INFRASTRUCTURE: underlying support, usually referring to the roads and other services provided to a community

INTERNAL COMBUSTION ENGINE: an engine powered by fuel burned inside of it, as opposed to in a separate external boiler

KEROSENE: a type of fuel for heating and lighting, made from refined petroleum

MOLDBOARD: the curved part of a plow, just behind the cutting edge, where the loosened soil lands and is turned aside

MONOCULTURE: devoting an entire farming operation to producing one crop

MONOPOLY: exclusive right to control the purchase and sale of specific goods or services

PETROLEUM: a liquid formed deep in the earth by the compression of organic matter over millions of years

PISTON: a disk or short rod made to closely fit in an engine cylinder so that changes in pressure inside the cylinder cause the piston to move. The motion of the piston is then used to drive machinery, such as the paddle wheel on a steamboat or the wheels of a locomotive.

PRAIRIE: grasslands, like those located in the American Midwest

REFINERY: a plant where crude petroleum is refined by removing impurities so that the refined products—such as gasoline, kerosene, paraffin, and heating oil—can be put to various uses

ROBBER BARONS: name given by journalists to extraordinarily wealthy, aggressive, unscrupulous, and successful American businessmen of the late nineteenth century

SHORT CIRCUIT: a weak point in an electrical circuit that causes the circuit to shut down if it is overloaded, thus preserving the rest of the power grid

SLUICE: a ditch or trough that carries slurry from a mine site to the point where miners extract the ore

SLURRY: mixture of water and soil

STEAM ENGINE: an engine that uses steam under pressure to produce power. In the most basic form of steam engine steam enters a cylinder and is then compressed with a piston.

VERTICAL INTEGRATION: control of all essential supply, production, shipping, and distribution functions by a single business

VOLATILE: rapidly evaporating and easy to ignite

WHIPSAW: a long, narrow handsaw set in a frame, used to cut wood along the grain (as opposed to a crosscut saw)

WINDROWS: the rows into which cut hay is raked to promote drying

ADDITIONAL RESOURCES

BOOKS:

Bridgman, Roger. *Inventions and Discoveries*. London: Dorling-Kindersley Publishing, 2002.

Ingpen, Robert, Robert R. Wilkinson, and Philip Wilkinson. *Encyclopedia of Ideas That Changed the World*. New York: Viking, 1993.

Jonnes, Jill. *Empires of Light: Edison, Tesla, Westinghouse, and the Race to Electrify the World*. New York: Random House, 2003.

Karwatka, Dennis. *Technology's Past: America's Industrial Revolution and the People Who Delivered the Goods*. Ann Arbor, MI: Prakken Publishing, 1996.

Macaulay, David. *The Way Things Work*. Boston: Houghton Mifflin Co., 1988.

Olsen, Byron and Joseph P. Cabadas. *The American Auto Factory*. St. Paul, MN: Motorbooks International, 2002.

Olson, James S. *Encyclopedia of the Industrial Revolution in America*. Westport, CT: Greenwood Press, 2002.

Wallace, Robert. *The Miners*. New York: Time-Life Books, 1976.

WEBSITES:

http://www.americaslibrary.gov
Select "Jump Back in Time"

http://www.fordham.edu/halsall/mod/modsbook14.html
Internet Modern History Sourcebook: Industrial Revolution – provides links to excerpts from historical texts

http://www.grc.nasa.gov/WWW/K-12/airplane/engopt.html
Simple and clear explanation of the four-stroke internal combustion engine

http://www.kidinfo.com/American_History/Industrial_Revolution.html
Links to numerous online reference resources

http://pbskids.org/wayback/tech1900/
About technology in America in 1900

SET INDEX

Bold numbers refer to volumes

PICTURE CREDITS

Author photo: 45 right; Colonial Williamsburg Foundation: 24, 60 right; *Frank Leslie's Illustrated Historical Register of the Centennial Exposition, 1876*: 5 bottom, 14 bottom; Ironbridge Gorge Museum Trust: 28 top, 60 top left; Library of Congress: Cover, Title page, 4, 8, 9, 10, 11, 12, 13, 14 top, 15, 20 top, 25, 26, 27, 28 middle, 28–29, 30, 30–31, 38 top, 39 top, 43, 44, 47, 49 bottom, 51, 52, 53, 54, 55 top, 56 top right, 57, 58–59, 60 bottom left, 61 bottom right, 62; McCormick Farm, Shenandoah Valley Agricultural Research and Extension Center, Virginia Polytechnic Institute: 19; National Archives: 6, 16–17, 18 top left, 20 bottom, 21, 22, 23, 34 top, 35, 36, 39 bottom, 41, 45 left, 46–47, 48, 49 top, 50–51, 55 bottom, 56 bottom left, 56 bottom right, 58 top, 61 left, 63; National Motor Museum: 33, 34 bottom, 37, 38 bottom, 40; National Museum of American History, Smithsonian Institution: 61 top right; National Park Service, Artist, L. Kenneth Townsend: 5 top, 18 top right, 18 bottom; Philadelphia Free Library: 56 top left